THE BOOK

OF LEAVENING

REBECCA GIVENS ROLLAND

Attention schools and businesses: for discounted copies on large orders, please contact the publisher directly.

For information contact:
Unsolicited Press
Portland, Oregon
www.unsolicitedpress.com
orders@unsolicitedpress.com
619-354-8005

Front Cover Design: Kathryn Gerhardt
Editor: Summer Stewart

ISBN: 978-1-956692-71-6

ACKNOWLEDGMENTS

Grateful acknowledgment is made to the editors of the journals and anthologies who first published the following poems, sometimes in earlier versions:

5X5: "Flares" (as "Next Stop Up"); *236 Magazine:* "Presence" (reprinted from *The Kenyon Review)*; *Barrow Street:* "Two in Winter"; *Bat City Review:* "This Eye and That"; *carte blanche:* "Colony"; *Connotation Press:* "Dream of Jaundice"; *Contemporary Verse 2:* "Women of Babylon" and "Goldenrod"; *Crab Creek Review:* "Song for Two Voices"; *Denver Quarterly:* "Dream of the Only Child"; *diode:* "Announcing," (now "Alchemy"), "Awaiting the First," and "The Tiny Feat"; *District LIT:* "Open, Near"; *DMQ Review:* "Octagon" and "Lean Times"; *Fourteen Hills:* "This Quantity of Light" (now "Solving for X"); *The Hampden-Sydney Poetry Review:* "Crumbs"; *The Hollins Critic:* "Arson"; *Hotel Amerika:* "Waystation for the Secretly Claustrophobic," "Near the Beachhead," and "A Hair Beyond"; *The Istanbul Review:* "Dream of Becoming"; *The Kenyon Review:* "Presence" and "Storm"; *Oxford Poetry:* "Rook-Edge" (Now "Song for the War Criminal"); *Poetry Northwest:* "Disclosure"; *REAL: Regarding Arts and Letters:* "After the Bee Sting" and "Openings"; *Silk Road:* "From the Book of Leavening"; *Stirring:* "After the Marriage But Before the Fire"; *Thrush Poetry Journal:* "After Visiting Hours" (now "After the Marriage but Before the Fire") and "Narrative of the Caveman Nearing Light"; *Verse Wisconsin:* "In the Hotel Lobby"; *Zone3:* "Birth Story" and "Song of the Ninth Month"

TABLE OF CONTENTS

THE BOOK

OF LEAVENING

I.

FAST FORWARD ONE HUNDRED YEARS

If what we spoke existed after us—
every phoneme flaring in fraught spirals

our voices turned votives: every hour
candling from windowsill to sea—

careful eyes veiling with cloud-threats,
throats gonging open vowels—

if one morning we witnessed neighbors
clambering over fields, enormous dogs

unleashed, upending clovers: Father
passing down decades of letters, weight

of scribbled envelopes in hand: if,
in that moment, we planed our heads back,

we'd find fortune in last casts of light: minds
steeled for coming years' constellations—

weft and weight of dust, galloping mares,
birthed pups, maned foals, mother caught

in a warren of bees—tail twitching, fast
flag, hooved beauties beyond, testing legs—

SONG OF THE CITIZEN FROM A PRIOR CENTURY

In our castle garden, a vagrant gust over ground
winds our ears like analog clocks. You stand your ground

alongside a sundial. Our gazebo gleams
where I left you, camellias wracked. Digging ground,

I find bulbs yet to bloom. Children long gone. Empty
yard beckons us to plant. We refuse. Lost, you ground

all our plans for now. Where was our treasure? Our
marked *X*? This map's useless, shows blank ground,

ghosts of women pinioned by hand-spinning
wheels for eternity. In memory's moat, I ground

heels, tell toes to flex, limbs to flutter. Yet, face
to face with you, I'm paralyzed. No king's ground,

this restrictive charter, more like a closed mouth,
wishing to open. Beg pardon? I demand red ground.

Come back, it begs. You'll freeze, find your feet. I
ask what other women want: guards to keep ground

from burning them whole, and no white fences? No.
How many years till tomorrow? Uncharted ground

from tick to tock, from snore to snore, from towel
to washcloth, souring with age: not the ground

I once said I'd give my life for. Not the countryside
I wanted to see. Will the two of us be ground

down together? Grow mad? Make symphonies?
Don't tell me I've loved you into the ground,

or haven't loved well. The ghost of an old regime
rises in me. I tap a new melody, gain ground.

PRESENCE

Bring on the unborn, the as-yet-
                   unreleased—let this body's sand-
trap convex, turn mechanism:
                   let throat's base beat
gold with the threat of steeped
                   branches, bleating,
tired till the hash
                   of rain no longer treads
lightly, thrushes hunger
                   fallowly abroad, chest thrums
tree-canopy's lashing in hurricane winds
              out the window—
domestic bliss? No: pockets of evening menace,
                   oiled scallions, roots
catalyze this pot into ash, this pan
                   into battle cry, banging
ceasingly the steel-cut
                   edge—let knees be a flicker
of over, feet find light sleep
                   under ribs—feet treading
the meadow in the hip of
presence, angled forward

till only grass, only field-rot,
finds blooms—now harkens,
multiplies to a thousand
entitlements of solitary
leaves—for once commands
gather forces, smack trouble, smatter
darkness into inner ear—

HUNGER AS THE ORDINARY ART

While dressing, I shut
                    the door: ashamed
at what I've come to   what has become
of this body   he once thought
made for love—

my husband enters: only a tiny
                                    insinuation
                freckled glance
at this corpus
        the whole
of the tongue-
tied body   its convex swerved
                        to meet convex
space where tiered lines
                        marking childbirth
                appear   space where
no human has
                for some time made
inroads   ramshackle
                plot
of fallow field
furrows interspersed

like no one else's   tricked-
out path   to him
lovemaking is nothing but
                    a second

language   he's fluent in
   no matter how disaffected   how distant
                    we've harrowed
and translated
this land   the outer folds

the inner folds   between them

                    famished   marriage
unspeakable space

SONG OF THE NINTH MONTH

Each of us invisible
to the other: fetus, you'll
push forward, glommed
against spine. Tinge
of movement in cartilage,
near heart chamber, subtly
under breath, wicking
spine. Your best bet: don't
let world's noise find you
too fast. Ecolocating,
your first embrace
of walls. Twinge of termites
gnawing inedible air. You
gobble all, unsatisfied.
Need's never enough
to fulfill you. You refuse
to survive on shadows, demand
more bread, more food,
alphabets of elegance, mistrust—
until, years later, I'll summon
you—hardened, having
learned to manage in distant
villages, cities of mango

and meat. Sweet lands: still
no one will greet you, flood you:
immense, welcoming. No
one will flush hunger
from your mouth. This
second, you kick forward—
no scars at ankles, no flecked
knees. At judges' feet, indelible
questions—was I not enough
without you? Not sufficient
without a second set of lungs? I
buy an extra suitcase—days
two-step, turn dangerous. Lungs
empty like luggage. Will I
be left with more than
your shed skin—will I
be more than a shrugged-off
shell that ocean echoes in? No
boundaries you won't
trespass, no burden you won't
suffer, slough off. What fierceness
you've already had to earn—

STORM

—as if the makeshift house
had finally flattened,
instantiation
of another, undimming light—
wind scavenging insulation,
eaves—locked ease
already splitting
                    to blared motion, nattering
deafness, the ear's split rind—
                    wracking flecks, mallowing
past haunches, wresting fallow
seed from fractured pools—
spent, we trap no more
than ordinary tornness, bleached
blousing cast from scoured
ties —soon we sweep the field on hands
and knees—what's left,
what mechanism,
each casement individual, reduced—
                    not everything can be rescued—
                    undermined—
not every stake rises
automatically—exclamations

sunder, even copper crusts over,

                    oxidizes, contains the last

of what it will not

contact—banisters flush to dead wood—consider us

no riven specimens, no filters scattered

to contorted dust—the wake

of us, the wreck we hardly see—

even birdsong flails

as bricks tumble to earth—even cross-

beams, meeting in branch-light,

mazing forward,

blister, unwillingly break—

FROM THE BOOK OF LEAVENING

I listen at times to backs of bread,
backs of books, fronts of hands. Listen
so long, I question if anyone courts
noise anymore. The valley's rude bee
hovers: glistening stinger. Obviously
knows me. Sour honey, sweet year. I keep
low in this sky-lit city. No wasps
welt my back. Dry air mists. Snow
snarls housefires. *Necessary,* I read, *water
for crops. Irritant wind to hang low.* I
translate your story: make the title
United, change it to *Questions of
Flight.* Summoned mid-sentence, I
shake, listen close at bedroom railings,
eaves. Close enough, my father's
whistling comes clear. *Get up,* he
commands, wet-cheeked, *time to attend
to every lost cause.* What can I do to love
the way I promised? All directions
funnel to shadow. Hours
of solitude find every wrinkle. Fury
rises: a choking miasma. Whenever
I listen, the next day removes itself, then

the next, till evenings sing themselves
to sleep, dig down impassable roads. Flags
span windows, brittle blue. Cloth flakes,
turns translucent, washed. Shuttered light
shifts winter warm. Railroads make
nations mobile, geography accessible, if
shifting's an actual promise. Toe
to heel. *Let's spread out together,* I hear
at the window, *praise what architecture
allows.* Father, Father, guard the mud,
watch the mud. Something about wick
of the candle, I want to say something
about trimming the lamp—*douse the wick,*
the lover cries, *it's almost morning.* Justice
or injustice, refuse retreat. Thoughtless,
my brother and I say, translating together,
granite in both our throats—we'll
extinguish lamps, no longer children,
will cry out, *heavy land, admonish us—*

BIRTH STORY TOLD THE SEVENTH TIME

you'll need talismans they said
don't forget they said

the hazel the greenwood
don't allow the child

to pull its own cord
swallow sound leaving this body

this hinge this muscle mouth don't
expect his cries to startle you

don't flee the violence of it
your frame heavier yet hollow

ruin of uninhabited moon
room a battery of beeps

child's first scores recorded
every name and number shouted

upending sound eager questions
thrumming: how will she drink

or breathe what miracle will drive
her onward from what country

has she arrived before swift cells
broke open: such white

muck such elusive squalls so
tender—who's airlifted her

from blank landscape to ours—
who alive has packed his

farewell jacket who has gone
and ripped the untouched cloth

NARRATIVE OF THE CAVEWOMAN NEARING LIGHT

Cost of conch shells rises like floodwaters:
memory of unmarried decades,

of sunlight on a child's
half-noticed face. Layers of sediment

I've tried not to let bury me, grainy irritants
collecting in bends, flecked with fool's gold,

mother braiding, three times over,
wet strands, then releasing, beckoning us

both up a never-seen hill—I've tried
not to let flashes upend me. No landscape

I can't abide. I dream instead
of neutral tenderness: wild orange

blossoms, sparrow-wings flicking
in patterns, pressed flesh, a white-

flecked peel. If I reckon long enough
with rinds, wearied blossoms, I'll catch

a weathervane flying by:
imported cloud-hung ramparts, memories

of someone else entirely: reeds
up to elbows, wading in sand dunes,
water lapping the backs of knees.
Civilization a keening, cracked vowel.

echoing in this modern-day cave,
where a match strikes my name—

the one no one knows—warming me,
while I deny bitter root's dragging—

no sign of drafted sheetrock, beams
sky-lit—only sunlit passage, ear's

sound-sap, echo of *world, world, word.*

DREAM OF JAUNDICE

I.
Newborn languishes under light-box: no one
taught her to search for sun. Eyes taped
shut, near-ecstatic, limbs infolded.

This doll-bed corrals her—torso's barreled
in elemental blue, cheeks striated
by clear tubes. Impeccable machines whir. *What*

an improvement—white coats check heels'
tint: typical? A more skin-like shade? Hours
question her patience, test mine. Monitors

stutter, short—count one breath, two. Flip
the gold switch: she's aged a decade. Imagine
ineloquent mutters: *feed pilgrims, water*

plants, be of use. Her childhood swept clean
of choices—while outside, caterpillars
swing and sway, alive only one month,

 flightless, swaddling each hanging leaf,
mimicking the mummies they inspired.

II.
Illumination—gold-scrolled, framed—
fails us. Doctors arrive without promised
cures. Still unborn, she's laid out, flatlined—

a passel rush in for the pulse—*deceleration*—
the best minds drop plans, hang heads. I'm
fluorescent, flaring, useless: a no-man's

land. Their decision: descend her overly
early. Devices muffle our cries in waiting
rooms. Once my lips chattered: once

I followed gauze-inflected orders. Now,
I await the drug meant to help her mature—
she kicks, bruises, swings. Pain's never

deterred her, sericulture lost after one
missed feeding. Liquid silk, sericin,
hardens on air's exposure, drops

in a golden-thread whorl. No way to lift
nets, to free her. Panel of interventions,
unopened hatch. Has she flown off?

Requested new disguises? Hours I watch—
mute vessel, muted witness—at once
I feel her, dream her, wing through air—

COLONY

As if grave inscriptions were enough, I plunge
my face in slate-riven water.
Given dense enough darkness, high tides,
I'll drown. What survival conceals itself
in tunnels? What contingencies linger
underground? I stand tall: weight shifts
from toe to fist, Neanderthal to agriculturalist,
to conference room. Time whirls. Settling
down: simpler than I imagined. This
landscape startles past, a pacific mood:
a passel of fish pass me. Clams jitter,
sacked. I've got no relation to this land's
language. No way to cram the right
word in. Soon exhaustion will hover,
rot whittle the supple banks of trees.
I'll exhaust myself, attempting speech. No
use imputing emotion—news will arrive,
tantrum, collapse into a whir of green
and red. Blotted signatures tear
off censored pages. For now, descent
weeps. Letters still unwritten haunt
me. Turned colonist, I cringe, assemble
passports. Squall-breath, festering

in my stomach, cleans me out. What
worth accrues to mud except in
silence. Silence turns every mad
word gold. No ruler able to mutter
answers. My body taken. Words
seek refuge. Quaking, the village green.

SEMAPHORE

Mid-morning: dust in full bloom—flicker
of fingernail—start anew, newly

barren—*phoenix, find me*—yet drenched
blinds cover windows—singed ash

smarts in chimneys—tattoos obscure
birch leaves' visible veins—I'm

veined, aged, battered by attempts
to intuit, to figure, to grieve—face gives

the impression of lost origami—papery,
fixed folds and wings—you peel layers

till bird flips to fly-away airplane—till
beak reframes itself as sky—at first

I tried no emotion—encoded fragrance
as log-wood for dye—not this

capsule of pollinated ocean—not
jacarandas' eager releasing—

not bare sex postponed—*listen*
we're not talking seeds sunk in water—

rather childbirth's lingering wound:
wise ones claim time scars over

with stronger skin; origami arms—
unfolding fights over nothing—bipinnate

leaves sway close, no destination—our
mouths blank messages, harrowing wind—

TWO IN WINTER

Let the heave of waking, levitating,
        break us. Let ashes deny
our elevated passion, bare throats
        caving in thirst: deny
hardwood need that sanctifies
        our hunger. Listen: to deny
our bodies' twinned reliquaries
        means no one's spared. Deny
sugar to horses, saints to sharp-faced
men, who can't deny
this drive to eloquence. Stream
        of reckless mouths—deny
sourdough, caramelized craving:
        sweet-sick, insomniac. Deny
morning's caught light, forbidden
        lovers—beheaded perennials deny
our one shot at spring. Penitent
flashes: past fires deny
our will for untethered lives, remind
with every breath, to deny
healing's steep price on our heads.
        Gamblers, we bid to deny
this country, poker-face our pack

of unsaid desires. Deny
bouncers mounting back staircases—
      I'll show my hand, deny
this full flush, these thirty potions
undrunk, unsaid. Deny
how wistful we've grown, hazy
final pleasures. No fault you deny
will be forgiven, no rash bet
will be believed. Slap *deny*
on strangers' wrists—hardheaded,
      paranoid. Anyone here? Deny
my final wager. I'll let song scar
this hidden camera. Deny
the click on flesh, flash on monogamy—
      in these territories, to deny
a woman is to rob the house, flee
her ghostly echoes: *here, deny.*

II.

DREAM OF THE DISAPPEARING CHILD

One month post birth: still I wonder
at her name's reverberation—
as I watch: have her cheekbones,
after trauma, slackened,
               ghostly? Has
her underworld face
aged prematurely? Will her gold foot,
cast, reek of heat in winter,
echoing sighs'
circumference? Crescent-moon-watcher, insomniac, I find
     myself
racking up rosaries, spinning
the night-swing
of beads—crackle
of cartilage, bones left
in waiting—a lady,
                       a darling, a dear—
let the bold eyes of her backbone
overtake her, let the beading
and unbeading
bring her in—

finally, sleep finds me: catching
the hooves
of five unburied
horses, hearing the clock under the river
snap its mane—

WHAT SURVIVAL MEANT

Wind stirs the book of dalliances—the first line's lost.
Husband finds his body strengthened: lover, lost.

Drained, we wake to cloudless sky: coupled, leafless.
Bad weather stops our burnt lungs, rained-out, lost.

Cymbals, red lights signal this land's unhinging—
Don't listen, we shout to Ursinus, maps we've lost.

Pebbles chart sidewalks. Birches drop bark like hints.
Bicyclists cross our cul-de-sac. You call, *Get lost.*

Look (I respond) *I touched him once. but never after.*
Will I forever be the blamed one, claim I'm lost?

Solitude meets the mind, later the gut. Thank god
for silent dinners, recipes even the best book lost.

I've stirred enough and learned enough of winter:
its pickled sticks, its Mozart, music its songbirds lost.

Needing you was what survival meant. It came well-
packaged, need and aftermath, wicked fire. *We're lost,*

I called twice over, stalled. But you didn't try
pretending: not in this charade, a poker game lost.

You have all you need for tomorrow?, ex-lover asks.
In her garden, I gather sweet stones, scout the lost,
Cry, *Don't go back.* I overleapt limbs, jigged mazurkas—
believe me, light inside was nothing like light I lost.

THIS EYE AND THAT

She is older, finally, old
enough not to be worried over,
ceding sleep. She is old enough
to moniker *girl*. On our couches,
on our long walks, we settle, older
than we remembered. When I sing, my voice catches
like a stuck latch where I stand
at the threshold, meeting
another insomniac midnight—
but I sing past my voice's crack,
the bough breaks as it was meant to
for the last centuries—
then I sleep, and darkness
between the thighs
ferries me down—
we chart our fury,
as it has come
to us through
our listening, squalling us—
no point pretending I don't
know what's brought them on.

Such abandon: soon, there's nothing

                    we can't argue about.

Every sentence shifts

              like quicksand. Vengeance fills

the mind's every corner—

in the muddiest

of chambers, behind

the separate bedrooms,

we hide our small griefs: the window

closed behind us,

the birds' wings

summoning, air uncleared—

whoever notices

the window's dust, whoever

              witnesses

its freckled

half-glass—take this child

                sitting with me

for ages of aging, in bare

                    silence sacred

rooms—*this is the eye*

that loved

you most, I say, *same*

eye that sweeps off nicked sky—

THE WOMEN OF BABYLON

When your mother and my mine were children
they kept wishing
for moths to alight
on their elbows

knife-nicks to pockmark their knees
equinoxes
of shadow to hasten
them past home   unmute mouths

let doves enunciate
missed syllables   gold dust-
storms settle their feet

rain on their bread's bitter crusts
breastmilk dried   as they aged
no angel carting flaming

sticks arrived   no letters consumed
them   no beds disappeared
into doorframes

old hatless men
        came to greet them   asking
for them to spin quiet dirges
            to bury names

white slips nobody wanted
worn inside out
dozens of years
husbands used to draw the line

at lilies   salamanders
everything they'd wanted
to stay left
formless   children
with heaving dark eyes
swallowed sound

ALCHEMY

Maternal torso
        cleaving under
elemental metals (potassium,
rubidium, cesium)
high-
pressure,
sloughing free—

tensed, compressed—high
conductivity—

weathering
patience
(malleable,
ductile,
dropping shells)

body-centered,
face-centered—
dread

of trapped
flames frightens

mother's sleight
of hand
saves: gold
leaf
in her
mouth
transmits green light.

DISCLOSURE

Late evening, metals bolstering our
houses finish acting like anything
but themselves. Bauxite, copper,

rods we bored under trees' aegis:
forgetting injected fluid, cracks in
unwitting steel. Years later, a landmine

excavates us—crack-seal veins
bubbling up, flaring out—formations
pressurized from inside. Silica lingers

in brushed air. Silos empty to wind,
grainy clouds we hardly see. Is breath
our only hopeful model? Is exhaling

our exit strategy? Sand has lied to us.
Irritants conquer our guts. We weep
frost. Our hungry children eat sky.

We recite *our wedding, their births,*
this fire, but snow covers us anyway:
our slit umbrella trickles visible rain.

Our play circles, losing rhythm.
One child rings rosies, shakes her shovel
in chemicals too cautious for palms. All

the world's time and money spent. Every
gold coin tail-flipped. Nothing to save.

ARSON

At my neighbor's house: no one said
          or knew anything. Everyone only
stood and watched it burn. Only one
          girl battered our door, crying
Help, and I ran to try. Refusing horror:
          a sign of resistance—refuting
the panic of fires everywhere. That night:
a cardinal clung to bare branches,
hoping for I know not what. I gnawed
my lip, wishing bad news could flush us
of unwanted anxiety, that worse news
would find the perpetrator, beating
a familiar cadence on victim's graves—
still ill at ease among these green-terraced,
impeccable homes—if only patience
were a debt, if I could pay it with bills
hoarded under the mattress—if only I could
work less for remembrance, memorial rock,
if I could lift off, manage

to break ties—that house still flaming,

pockmarked, as I hasten

toward it, dreaming, doors razed almost off

                            this hinge of light—

AFTER THE MARRIAGE BUT BEFORE THE FIRE

Lovers once—nights like bandages stripped off,
minding one child—ten years married off.

Our castle has ten windows, eleven curtains.
Which view eyes storm-towers? Close it off.

Entrapped, I dared your darts. Caught
in this keep, you begged escape. I buzzed off.

Scientific defenses—flanking fire, moats—
kept us careful. *Timber!*, I cried, nodding off.

Husbanding strength behind palisades, I sipped
the contrite sop you offered, ticked off.

This season, we suffer outer walls, enceinte—
no internal holds, you whisper, tip me off.

You gave me a glass watch that never fastens,
whose slow ticking dares me: cast it off.

Will you profess desire—an instant—before
retaliating? Confess: I'll strip clothes off.

No stones for our daughter: she loves planes
that tilt wings, lose their balance, tumble off.

Ten years married. Memorize that much.
 I'll fire once—you'll betray me—stagger off—

barbed mouth crenelated, lips scoured off?
My name's upended, last vowels hastened off.

SOLVING FOR *X*

Will our daughter
stay solitary? Will another
enter this body, fill
for a second time this frame,
                     this tomb? This
room's
an onion peeled
for revelation, reveling
       in tossed seeds, goldenrod debris—
if for some reason
X is impossible to notice—
if daughter
and mother could
hunger for thirty years,
and still need no one—
         remain
perennial, enough for each other—
two cleaved seeds—
               you are enough—

husband's bare language—

                              are fine—

fine, as a vase is fine, broken—

As she sleeps,
I try to write a letter—
insisting on the quantity of syllables—
envying
hours' Niagara
rushing over—if another
bird emerges
from an egg,
they'll shift
positions in the nest,
making
room—

OCTAGON

What they call birth, this body empty
as a tomb. If, in this open-field
flesh (vector,
magnetic,
field of sets) I try to see clear: a widow
spider, torn filaments flapping
      like a flag in wind—if, in the expanse
                    of clanging night,
my child's first sobs rise,
endless, flexing my spine, reverberating
in wounded womb—if, on a brief walk,
my torso's arches
      sally open,
bones plucked
      from bridged back,
cherry-
tree knees,
              light
chapping brink of bricked
clavicle,
      if my child's face flickers

up at mine—webbing between
my palms catches,
      froglike at water's
edge, appearance
       of smoothness
relinquished, mandible
rescinded, dreams
                    traceless,
      reminding
of fossilized pre-natal back story—
                 but then a gurgling
laugh stops my laboring, girding
for green leaves, betraying
illusions of singular mind

AND YET RESOUNDING

in darkness we're human containers   of
resounding
unspeakable grief   that finds us (gold-braceleted)
entombs us   won't retreat

in darkness   our need for escape sizzles
in pots with flecked eggs we still smell
in spark-riddled trains   commuters locked in sear-
light

shade striping the passenger sides   resplendent
in the mind's Chinoiserie   before evening
collapses on us we fight against visible moons

lose tickets in conductor-less cars   each man a
shadow
as landscapes plane open to greenwood glory
each woman rehashing body's recoil   lingering in birth-

light as we might   its bookend death once again
river irrigates the insistent song one errant rock
diverts the path   three thousand years

sleep in the heat   of deepest earth

air will be clamored for

battled over   breeding unnecessary deaths

WAYSTATION FOR THE SECRETLY CLAUSTROPHOBIC

You, ex-lover, stay silent. The window billows sound.
Post-child, I'm mummified: you listen, make no sound.

I've developed last year's pictures, but see no face.
The leap from not-here to here—do you catch sound?

Fall in the city, I beg for leaves, catch only trapped air.
How does air feel in embalmed hearts—like sound?

Will I no longer travel? Will every mother-curse find me?
Cotton-mouthed, you know me by touch, not sound.

Offered spices, palm wine, rest, I demurred, murmured.
Which organs could you hook, dry, drain for sound?

Natron-dipped, my heart's jarred, tongue liquified.
Opposing rituals preserve us. Seized breaths sound.

Threat of moist air, ruin, closes in. We're the trusted ones:
in shadow-houses, we visit, chatter, impress with sound.

Forty days, I've wept: *Should we have another?* No one answers. Afterlives, glass-green, smatter with sound.

I guard our child with amulets. *Overprotective*: my curse. Your face shifts: restless, you seal up, raveling sound.

I do: that long-ago vow, once familiar, eviscerates. I've lost its rich gong. *Call me Janus*: switch off the sound.

OATH TO AN EARLIER SELF

A dream of near night:
I've ridden too far
afield. Bridle path,

the river erodes— nine months
reign, rain, and rein me—
bit between my teeth. No

cattails or dovetails—just
unseen glass-beaded
aspens. Advanced

maternal age: sun-shards
filter, face golds, back
seizes—I tread uphill. How

long have I lied:
self-sufficient? Not land
I meant to ride on:

eroded past recognition.
Who's to blame
in this country of *too old*—

tidal flats, flooded
embankments? How long
can I claim any innocence?

Blue-tipped wings angle off,
find distance—slow bird's
devoured. Child cries: migration

to strange skies, scarred
attachments—
snow, shadow, claws.

AFTER THE BEE STING

Near evening: I've lost patience, swift
pattering of mother to child: *Let's go*

home, I sally out, sheep with my lips
shut tight, poor belly with nothing to lose—

go home, the rest of the herd will
be tallied tomorrow. Back, we're no
better. Have the table legs always

fought with mine? Does the toddler always
tumble, flail, return to standing,

incessantly—did these questions
always shutter windows' craned-open

panes, fill me with startling grief? Once,
stones annotated my palm, as an abacus

ballasts counting, no one asks
if secrets boomerang, aerofoils spin

curved flight, games I know, but stay
zip-lipped about. I scowl, delinquent,

never dear. *No*—the child won't notice:
pepper-mad, unaware, he sets stones

on my shoulder to claim. They drop
without impact: he heaves them, fires

elliptical flight, giving me reasons
not to cycle back. These are the weapons

I've warned him of: I'm barren again,
blank as a wheezing woman,

and he's still a ghost of a boy.

III.

THE HOUSE WITH THE BRIGHT LOCKED DOOR

We once called it guilt   nameless morning
green ease summoning   shirred-off light

disputes over   who weighed flag's forty stars
who cleaned the chimney   who hosted

this heart best   this heart's beast   sheer ice
flitters at eaves   calves away   ephemeral

oaks ask *have you tried hard*   grafted branches
constantly forgetting   wind's accidental

pressure in lark-leaf space   between drips
of winter-worn roof   our neighbor's

always clearer than ours   you wash
hands' backs   this day   refuse adornment

weightless   blue taffeta cloth   claim sky's
ours as we invisibly   age toward invisible

every year we try not to tally   and fail
who's had time for thought   silence gifted

today   swallowed tomorrow   cumulus

stops up all argument   ash leaves

refuse to tremble   we know their reasons
as we know this day's edges   aren't ours

IN THE NIGHT MIRROR

Blunt the axe, initial the weapons: call the war good.
What starts in the mind stays in the mind for good.

A pearl from my necklace, dropped string: you noticed
nothing. War on, you strung up promises, none good.

Night's underside, packed bags: no man travels simply.
Crushed, I dreamed of cherries: weightless, good.

Music's echo startles, staunches blood: you've heard it?
Take this forest, its berries half poisonous, half good.

Meals you've eaten perish as soon as you swallow.
Sweet roots slide into your belly, its loops no good.

I'll never find a flower riper than the one I offer you
now: this morning, a faithful priestess, making good.

Once your women launched empires: now, they guard
temples, sulking. Columns stutter: the going's good.

Architecture's shot, the scaffolds deceptive. Repeat
after me—we're migrants, mercenaries (*it's all good*).

The weight of war undoes the emperor's claims. Lost,
I ask what you demand of us: the wrong, the good?

For now, finality's unmentionable: it's still just spring.
Summer, reasonable daughter, gathers what's good.

If we win this war, say, will I get clearance? Will breath
slap the spared man's lungs, turn these laws good?

Sometimes, in the night mirror, I catch my face's ghost.
When it breaks, there's no solace, not one edge good.

Tonight you'll say I'm loose-lipped. I'll hardly argue.
I'll be the mad one if you let me. Don't ask if I'm good.

PORTRAIT OF THE WARTIME LIVING ROOM

Voiceless, you squall at lamplight; I don't speak.
Not even the waiters, not even the doormen speak.

Caught in promises, harried blessings, you hurried
out, singed your words twice over, stopped to speak.

Strung up, I've caught you cursing, head to ground:
you demanded cymbals, phrases I couldn't speak.

This flower's always lovelier in shadow: I admit it.
Drained, you scurry from our bedroom as we speak.

Finding its flame, exhaustion flings us backward—
does backlashed wind still sear us, make us speak?

Half-stunned, half-gladdened, I find my hurt spine
shaken. Fear the cost, the shine, that asks to speak.

If tomorrow's your last, would you claim patience?
Would this landscape sweep up rubble, never speak?

I report what I can, I see what I say—it's madness.
No rock in the shoe, no death in the city will speak.

Yet still the day planes forward with open beak,
carrying sackcloth, breathing in: our talons speak.

Our gods we toss, stick by stone: wilderness falls.
Landscape's clogged with detritus. We walk and speak.

At your bedroom, I demanded where my child went.
Barefoot, you rushed backwards, refused to speak.

Is this our loss, have we guzzled this unborn city?
The day shifts cleanly by: the last guards speak.

Can this sad song defect? Road smacks of ocean.
Whistling, I'll say nothing, let the teakettle speak.

OCULAR

Sleep now. Only two words—my husband's—
not ill-intended, in late
afternoon: then
the scored
lash
     of exhaustion drops
me, eye-
wings creased
in the pit
         of a half-
aching head. My poor vision
         has worsened.
My first weariness, that of travelers
    sans drink, *sans*
rest. All I imagine is when
the fatigue will end. And always,
those flooding cries, seeking
         moisture,
or dryness—haunting
even out of sight
      or mind. What terrible

trespass lives

                    in oceans we haven't

encountered, what gongs

echo heavily

in seawalls,

over waves. Is that

the sound of my

breathing, or hers?

My need, or hers? Breathe

in depths

                        of another

insatiable morning—

                waking, stiff, my husband and I

stumble out of what

we thought

                to be light. A brief glance

out the living-room windows: winged

burden of tinged

                    feathers

torqued—

each molted tuft, each

                gallery of white

ravishes ripples,

                  grieving

lost knowledge,

whatever

      scars we can

            remember. I beg

the bird to flit in, to comfort

us, the way I must comfort:

            endlessly. The bird

does not enter. Cannot enter. Its wings

      beat once, twice—a harried

flapping—then it hastens

            away. I turn back

to my husband. The room seems,

all of a sudden, so small. If one pass over

         these married lives turns

to frost—

a silver spiraling down—each

weary bones hang

      like a mobile, spun

         by unseen air. What

have we done, making that lifelong

         promise? Ocular

vision has left, will

      leave

us. If ever

      fire beneath

         our feet

claims us, hastens
us forward,   if ever wind
strums
the bridge
of all we mourn, I won't claim
        surprise—
we'll sleep
under veils, in separate
rooms, the child
unaware,   our minds
suspended,
remembering air's
swift notes, bird's singular thrumming—

A HAIR BEYOND

At sea's edge, a party
            of three: mother, father,
daughter. Each of us
            I imagine with only
those names, two syllables
            at the Atlantic's edge: Crane's Beach,
 whose namesake beauties we've yet to see,
though sun breaks impeccably
            over us. We've
made it to a six-month daughter. Clean
space between mother and child. I
            breathe in, breathe
for what feels the first time, fill
            buckets we've brought
for her. Water spills out, cool relief
            over fingers, seeps
            into sand rising to dunes'
extravagant waving grasses. In this
half-unfamiliar
landscape fraught with shadow,
            light, and frothing surf,

I have no doubt
            light has struck
again   the weight
        of light
whose demands no longer seem burdensome—
salt-rimmed hands clap—
                    seafaring birds pass

unnoticed, as we pass
        the dinner hour entranced—
as air darkens ocean to lead
    and wind gusts
                dusk-
gutted light pants and cuts—I long
        for its source, for our lives' second
half—for the child's
dappling breath
misting me
            with future memory—

SONG FOR TWO VOICES

Say the curtained child drums complaints

two-four hunger   no matter   no time

for symphonies   say my vowels flame in

and out her right ear   over treble eyelids

high to low pitch   swift backbeat   sweet dread

say I carry clefts nestle bass lines   fermatas

refuse to let her cries   grow allegro

leaving one upended whimper   out to dry

six weeks pass   I grow weary   a single
violinist

sans score   no hope of coda   last row

I startle to notice   bass shadows

branched   against our windows   the child's throat

swaddled   orchestral sheets   she stutters

falters   finds her own music   what we'll sing her

when she's older   if she asks

DREAM OF THE AILING MOTHER

Was I once golden?—post-child, now
satiated—
lights on me bluer than breath—
jaundiced, the way my daughter
                        was—jaundice,
in the dream, meaning death—only three hours
to say
goodbye—whetting
thief's tongue,
stealing off—
costly diagnosis—*you've loved*
mortal things too much—
                        won't attendants
take me soon, won't my next meal
nourish, stop this sickness, stir
growth—time
for silent thought   impossible—
I rehearse lost words:
alfalfa, milk
thistle, nettle—I'll kneel
in fields, memorize lost names—

so domestic, these final
hours: rose
bulbs, windowless plant—
in this hospital, skin's ever

                              yellower—I'm
clothed in white—no
shrouds have anything on me—hardly
claimed, hardly
a clamshell
 more—my cry,
whiplashed, rescinds—reckoning
  remains my beck
and call—then: there she is: the child

                        at the window: shuttling me
to aftermath
of days—I'll live for her, for the chance

                        of her greeting
cherry-picked coasts,
oceans as yet unseen—
I'll think nothing of it, heal
my own wounds,   simultaneously
myself and a catalyst—

POSTSCRIPT FOR THE UNBORN

What if ocean loops its last waves
before you arrive: if lost ship's
wreckage surfaces, clear sightlines
      drawn, then lost
for good, and willingly: if night
      tells you of its constellations, lost
miles between mast and North Star:
you'd telescope, lost
to horizons of sheer wind, azimuth
measured clockwise, lost
days of your life still uncounted, fled
      to black. What if, lost
in a wintery ocean, you refused
to call me mother, make amends—lost
without the Dog Star, blank
compass you found, then lost,
Janus-faced, in white walls? I'd promise
to love better: no matter—energy lost
in fear of losing you, entropy, distress—
you kick, send up signals of lost
comfort, Morse-code signs of leaving:

in a month I'll be ghostly, lost
in waking-sleep spirals, driven
        to capsize. Exposed, lost
keel, turning turtle, mast down—
I follow your rolls. Whistling, *lost*
child, your dream, your first, your father
finds wisdom in you, lost
to any interrogation, Swiss clock
        of mind seeking sleep, lost
to jacklines, tethers, refusing
        entrapment—staying lost
to distance, you'll wake only to dream,
        luminescent shores lost
to lookouts. Eyes on you, I'll check
if green sap flares, if death's lost
power. No: reeling his lead-line, he'll
flip his heels: no matter lost
depths, no matter wrecks, forget
        lives your silent brothers lost—

SONG FOR THE WAR CRIMINAL

You're scar-cheeked, knees purled—trucks out
in force, guns tethered—beside, soldiers face out

to coke-bottle sky. Parroting charges, blameless,
gold-badged officer signals, *Stop*. Keep me out

of trouble, unaware, I beg. Packed traffic flares,
no destination—drivers panic, spin wheels, out

of luck. A decade of fingers point, release. Blind
curves: birds slap windows. Feathers I seek out:

trashed. Friends fall: mine. Wracked, I won't weep.
Elegies hide emotions. Speech needles the stings out

of laws. After ten years: what traction? Mind drums,
deliberate. Air: Anglo-Saxon. Your throat lets out

Germanic vowels. Seeking solace, I brood. Wanton,
trapped on snared roads, you accuse me, back out:

no hearing, no trial. You let go garden rows you promised
to remove, cities you visited, passport pages stamped out

of order. Lying, lied to (your final report), but I cling
to old tenderness. I'll let floods lose out

to drought, clean scuffed beaches of pebbles. Your
silhouettes I'll paint a dozen times. Fashioned out

of ink, this garden singes. I rake up, settle stones.
Forget the wake tomorrow: I'll send word out.

SONG OF CRUMBS

Massed clouds face
blue-backed windows—sky as bird

with no sense of self. Mornings,
we'll gaze out, myopic—

tire-treads trace impacted roads
out of this dying town. Clinging ticks

are all we'll find in wilderness. Losses
mark crescents, scar our backs.

We seek crumbs for succor,
spent laws to satisfy. Startled

speechless, we scour curtains, mumble
of curved horizons. We commit

to only so much, to such lush
seeing—then, even slick horizons

taper off. *Perilous,* a word
we won't repeat. Death a silver

handle we grab, held close
as brothers sharing rooms. Inner

hunger sharps our waiting throats.

False island cuts off, leaves us

witless as nattering toucans,
listening to someone's birthday music,

humming our wrecking song. None
of this has to do with us.

Not even our hapless candles, bread
cut, crustless, a coddled tale. Starved,

respectful, we praise this strong-arm
country. Grief won't distinguish

between us—we'll pass salt
at dinner, before lights surround us,

break fasts after wiping our mouths.
What else to do with this tenderness,

this knowledge, dark-pocked gifts
they keep trying to take away? We'll eat,

leave nothing, only traces too small
to sweep clean, or those we accidentally

scatter, step over not remembering.

SPILL

Watching the toddler learn to walk—
steps shoeless, falls back clown-like, leaves

her station, only to drop, belly first,
to the floor. Late morning: leaves

brushed against the windowpane,
painterly, serrated, wood-cut

by caterpillar ants. Watching the toddler
stand silent, a second, none

of her usual laughs or squalls, trying
to figure out how two legs should go. This

space of quietude, of the way we
function, or could, when our bodies

begin remembering what to do, through
collective unconscious examples:

ponytailed women jogging the park,
or talking or bored, kids splashing

in fountains, teenagers riding bikes
like broncos—which must look

to her like incredible machines—
clocks rocking forward, one hand

jolting faster than the other, as the day
brightens around us, as we struggle

to separate this moment from the next,
like distinguishing freckles and ticks,

vines from thorny brambles, waiting
till pricks' pain diminishes, till the pepper

is washed out with honey, till the ache

in the limbs starts to lift, till the hunger
of the body dims: summer,

the body knows, is a time of healing,
flushing wounds, soaking the splinter till

it surfaces to vision; reliving the miscarriage,
so vividly her eyes almost don't see—

her toddler learning to walk, watching cousins
grab her and lift her up—summer,
once abstract, becomes tactile:
wind brushing hot skin, cooling sweat;

a summons, a need clamoring to stay
upright, the will of the body, once

hidden, fully and viscerally known.

THE MOVIE, THE LAKE

You emerge from the lake   a silent movie
eyes crossed as you're carried away

crawl space in the crest of your ear
echoes of unmoored consonants drifting

heedless as meal after meal you startle
vanquishing hunger   disbanding need

mouth ballooning light   lips scrolling
through air's filmic grain   each word

subtitled   you might have spoken
each claim in double-time   promising

relief   the day I don't listen is the day
I'll regret   waving my Charlie flag

sailing into your mouth like Jonah
hungry in the hollow of your stomach

as you cry *foul* and *please release me*
no honest way to deny   no will to say no

I bless you   soothe you   wait
for the rolling credits   listening

to the fan's indelible music   watching
sleep drop its cloth over your face

FROM THE TERMINAL STATION

Say you listen till all blasts finish,
leaving no single human to listen,

no echo to hasten from us. Single train
pinwheels. Third-rail tracks. I can't listen:

these pneumatics shutter their lines. A cast
of vehicles, rope-hauled, propel us. Listen

to tracks' mad ghosts, upended. From
Latin *to pull*: I'll cling to motion, listen

as we're effaced. Blame our dim-lit table,
these half-drunk glasses. Railroaded, listen

to unhappy pendulums, fairy-tale gold
swung at a dead man's chest. I listen.

When I turn, he escapes, wrists trailing rope.
Rooster-crow. Nearing defeat, I listen:

grief ties me up, lassoes the last man out.
Will soldiers flex past with steel feet? Listen

for shelling of land. Give me decades,
not hours, to toss these blooms. Let me listen

to war's surface, flags above bones. I kneel
at echoes' edges. I hear, I pass on. Listen
at doorways—copy battle markers, arrows,
highlighted sparks. Is this our hope? To listen

requires nun's patience, sparrow-ears. Pullman
cars, sumptuous, let us sleep—bleary, listen

to tickets validated, twice stamped.
Refusal's cost crests over: concession? Listen,

I'll turn back if you will. Say what? No deal?
Tell me—justice, this black widow, will listen.

GOLDENROD

Mid-winter, I lean into darkness: ten times
over, I sing madrigals, sign cards. Sweet times—

I take out photos—find me: birds' wings, radial
syntax of carpus, metacarpus, alula. Digits of times

I've watched them brighten, spin—the clock's
a scattered sparrow, keeled for seeds, nine times

out of ten finding none—now, the muscles used
for flight unhinge and falter, tiny bones mark times

the eye's looked low, the skull's aspects unfuse,
whistles hasten to bones. Relatives dead: lean times

sliver off the intertarsal joint, synsacrum, coracoid
and scapula, wishbone. I won't cry. Birds in times

of drowning: flightless—winged birds shift
weight, bellow air into dead space. Even times

of grief glimmer in sternums, elongate the ossified
unknowns. I shiver: amniotic fluid marks times

of birth, of dappled, arrowing exit. Spring will find
us: I'll witness, will brave it, singe and land ten times

over ice, past stone. Outside, birds flap wings. Dark
nights double up, weightless, lacking teeth. Times

for weeping coincide with danger: gardens, beaks
hide the arrival of flames. Funerals. I've wiped times

tables from my mind, razorbills from my repertoire—
each day, I wake to scales, claws, spurs. If

hundred-mile increments of hope are left unfinished,
don't think migration's lost. I wake, stretch, echo times

of gliding, hasten on spring: I'll fast forget (caudal,
cranial) this sightline, these shell-hatching times.

ABOUT THE AUTHOR

Rebecca Givens Rolland is the author of three poetry collections, including *The Wreck of Birds* (Bauhan Publishing, 2012), winner of the May Sarton New Hampshire Prize. She teaches at the Harvard Graduate School of Education and works as a speech-language pathologist. She lives in Boston, Massachusetts.

ABOUT THE PRESS

Unsolicited Press is based out of Portland, Oregon and focuses on the works of the unsung and underrepresented. As a womxn-owned, all-volunteer small publisher that doesn't worry about profits as much as championing exceptional literature, we have the privilege of partnering with authors skirting the fringes of the lit world. We've worked with emerging and award-winning authors such as Shann Ray, Amy Shimshon-Santo, Brook Bhagat, Kris Amos, and John W. Bateman.

Learn more at unsolicitedpress.com. Find us on twitter and instagram.

www.ingramcontent.com/pod-product-compliance
Lightning Source LLC
Chambersburg PA
CBHW031440120626
46545CB00006B/2492

* 9 7 8 1 9 5 6 6 9 2 7 1 6 *